CONQUISTADOR

BOOKS BY ARCHIBALD MacLEISH

Archibald MacLeish

CONQUISTADOR

BOSTON AND NEW YORK

HOUGHTON MIFFLIN COMPANY

The Riverside Press Cambridge

FIRST IMPRESSION, MARCH, 1932
SECOND IMPRESSION, MARCH, 1932
THIRD IMPRESSION, APRIL, 1932
FOURTH IMPRESSION, FEBRUARY, 1933
FIFTH IMPRESSION, MAY, 1933
SIXTH IMPRESSION, JULY, 1934

The Riverside Press
CAMBRIDGE · MASSACHUSETTS
PRINTED IN THE U.S.A.

DEDICATION

'O frati,' dissi, 'che per cento milia
Perigli siete giunti all' occidente'

THE DIVINE COMEDY
INFERNO, *canto* XXVI, *lines* 112, 113

NOTE

WHERE I have followed the historical chronicles of the Conquest of Mexico I have, in general, followed the account given by Bernál Díaz del Castillo, one of the Conquerors, in his *True History of the Conquest of New Spain.* I have however altered and transposed and invented incidents at my own pleasure. I am indebted to the excellent notes of Mr. Alfred Percival Maudsley in his (Hakluyt Society) edition of the *True History.* My account of the topography of the march from the sea-coast to the Valley of Mexico is based upon my own experience of the route and the country by foot and mule-back in the winter of 1929 and differs from that of the historians. Indian names have been given their Spanish pronunciation for obvious reasons. (Professor John Hubert Cornyn's *Song of Quetzalcoatl* has a note on Aztec pronunciation for those who are interested.) Proper names have been accented for the reader's convenience even when no accent would be required in Spanish. I hope that the strength of my attachment to the country of Mexico may, to some degree, atone for my presumption, as an American, in writing of it.

The poem was written in 1928, 1929, and 1931 in Paris, Jalapa. and Conway, Massachusetts.

Bernál Díaz' Preface to his Book was published, in an earlier form, in the *Yale Review*, winter of 1929–1930, under the title 'Conquistador.'

CONQUISTADOR

PROLOGUE

AND the way goes on in the worn earth:

and we (others) —

What are the dead to us in our better fortune?
They have left us the roads made and the walls standing:
They have left us the chairs in the rooms:

what is there more of them —

Either their words in the stone or their graves in the land
Or the rusted tang in the turf-root where they fought —
Has truth against us?

(And another man

Where the wild geese rise from Michigan the water
Veering the clay bluff: in another wind....)

Surely the will of God in the earth alters:

Time done is dark as are sleep's thickets:
Dark is the past: none waking walk there:
Neither may live men of those waters drink:

And their speech they have left upon the coins to mock us:
And the weight of their skulls at our touch is a shuck's weight:
And their rains are dry and the sound of their leaves fallen:

(We that have still the sun and the green places)
And they care nothing for living men: and the honey of
Sun is slight in their teeth as a seed's taste —

What are the dead to us in the world's wonder?
Why (and again now) on their shadowy beaches
Pouring before them the slow painful blood

Do we return to force the truthful speech of them
Shrieking like snipe along their gusty sand
And stand: and as the dark ditch fills beseech them

(Reaching across the surf their fragile hands) to
Speak to us?
                    as by that other ocean
The elder shadows to the sea-borne man

Guarding the ram's flesh and the bloody dole....

Speak to me Conquerors!
                    But not as they!
Bring not those others with you whose new-closed

(O Brothers! Bones now in the witless rain!)
And weeping eyes remember living men:
(Not Anticlea! Not Elpenor's face!)

Bring not among you hither the new dead —
Lest they should wake and the unwilling lids
Open and know me — and the not-known end!

And Sándoval comes first and the Pálos wind
Stirs in the young hair: and the smoky candle
Shudders the sick face and the fevered skin:

And still the dead feet come: and Alvarádo
Clear in that shadow as a faggot kindled:
The brave one: stupid: and the face he had

Shining with good looks: his skin pink:
His legs warped at the knee like the excellent horseman:
And gentleman's ways and the tail of the sword swinging:

And Olíd the good fighter: his face coarse:
His teeth clean as a dog's: the lip wrinkled:
Oléa — so do the winds follow unfortune —

3

Oléa with the blade drawn and the clinging
Weeds about him and the broken hands:
And still they come: and from the shadow fixes

Eyes against me a mute armored man
Staring as wakened sleeper into embers:
This is Cortés that took the famous land:

The eye-holes narrow to the long night's ebbing:
The grey skin crawls beneath the scanty beard:
Neither the eyes nor the sad mouth remember:

Other and nameless are there shadows here
Cold in the little light as winter crickets:
Torpid with old death: under sullen years

Numb as pale spiders in the blind leaves hidden:
These to the crying voices do not stir:
So still are trees the climbing stars relinquish:

And last and through the weak dead comes — the uncertain
Fingers before him on the sightless air —
An old man speaking: and the wind-blown words

Blur and the mouth moves and before the staring
Eyes go shadows of that ancient time:
So does a man speak from the dream that bears his

Sleeping body with it and the cry
Comes from a great way off as over water —
As the sea-bell's that the veering wind divides:

(And the sound runs on the valleys of the water:)

And the light returns as in past time
                              as in evenings
Distant with yellow summer on the straw —

As the light in America comes: without leaves....

THE FIRST PART

BERNÁL DÍAZ' PREFACE TO HIS BOOK

BERNÁL DÍAZ' PREFACE
TO HIS BOOK

'THAT which I have myself seen and the fighting'....

And I am an ignorant man: and this priest this
Gómara with the school-taught skip to his writing

The pompous Latin the appropriate feasts
The big names the imperial decorations
The beautiful battles and the brave deceased

The onward marches the wild Indian nations
The conquests sieges sorties wars campaigns
(And one eye always on the live relations) —

He with his famous history of New Spain —
This priest is a learned man: is not ignorant:
And I am poor: without gold: gainless:

My lands deserts in Guatemala: my fig-tree the
Spiked bush: my grapes thorns: my children
Half-grown: sons with beards: the big one

Breaking the small of his back in the brothel thills
And a girl to be married and all of them snarling at home
With the Indian look in their eyes like a cat killing:

And this Professor Francisco López de Gómara
Childless; not poor: and I am old: over eighty:
Stupid with sleepless nights: unused to the combing of

Words clean of the wool while the tale waits:
And he is a youthful man: a sound one: lightened with
Good sleep: skilled in the pen's plaiting —

I am an ignorant old sick man: blind with the
Shadow of death on my face and my hands to lead me:
And he not ignorant: not sick —

                    but I

Fought in those battles! These were my own deeds!
These names he writes of mouthing them out as a man would
Names in Herodotus — dead and their wars to read —

These were my friends: these dead my companions:
I: Bernál Díaz: called del Castíllo:
Called in the time of my first fights El Galán:

I here in the turn of the day in the feel of
Darkness to come now: moving my chair with the change:
Thinking too much these times how the doves would wheel at

Evening over my youth and the air's strangeness:
Thinking too much of my old town of Medina
And the Spanish dust and the smell of the true rain:

I: poor: blind in the sun: I have seen
With these eyes those battles: I saw Montezúma:
I saw the armies of Mexico marching the leaning

Wind in their garments: the painted faces: the plumes
Blown on the light air: I saw that city:
I walked at night on those stones: in the shadowy rooms

I have heard the chink of my heel and the bats twittering:
I: poor as I am: I was young in that country:
These words were my life: these letters written

Cold on the page with the split ink and the shunt of the
Stubborn thumb: these marks at my fingers:
These are the shape of my own life....
                                        and I hunted the

Unknown birds in the west with their beautiful wings!

Old men should die with their time's span:
The sad thing is not death: the sad thing

Is the life's loss out of earth when the living vanish:
All that was good in the throat: the hard going:
The marching singing in sunshine: the showery land:

The quick loves: the sleep: the waking: the blowing of
Winds over us: all this that we knew:
All this goes out at the end as the flowing of

Water carries the leaves down: and the few —
Three or four there are of us still that remember it —
Perish: and that time's stopt like a stale tune:

And the bright young masters with their bitter treble
Understanding it all like an old game!
And the pucker of art on their lips like the pip of a lemon! —

'The tedious veteran jealous of his fame!'
What is my fame or the fame of these my companions?
Their tombs are the bellies of Indians: theirs are the shameful

Graves in the wild earth: in the Godless sand:
None know the place of their bones: as for mine
Strangers will dig my grave in a stony land:

Even my sons have the strangeness of dark kind in them:
Indian dogs will bark at dusk by my sepulchre:
What is my fame!   But those days: the shine of the

Sun in that time: the wind then: the step
Of the moon over those leaf-fallen nights: the sleet in the
Dry grass: the smell of the dust where we slept —

These things were real: these suns had heat in them:
This was brine in the mouth: bitterest foam:
Earth: water to drink: bread to be eaten —

Not the sound of a word like the writing of Gómara:
Not a past time: a year: the name of a
Battle lost — 'and the Emperor Charles came home

'That year: and that was the year the same
'They fought in Flanders and the Duke was hung —'
The dates of empire: the dry skull of fame!

No but our lives: the days of our lives: we were young then:
The strong sun was standing in deep trees:
We drank at the springs: the thongs of our swords unslung to it:

We saw that city on the inland sea:
Towers between: and the green-crowned Montezúma
Walking the gardens of shade: and the staggering bees:

And the girls bearing the woven baskets of bloom on their
Black hair: their breasts alive: and the hunters
Shouldering dangling herons with their ruffled plumes:

We were the first that found that famous country:
We marched by a king's name: we crossed the sierras:
Unknown hardships we suffered: hunger:

Death by the stone knife: thirst: we fared by the
Bitter streams: we came at last to that water:
Towers were steep upon the fluttering air:

We were the lords of it all....
                                    Now time has taught us:
Death has mastered us most: sorrow and pain
Sickness and evil days are our lives' lot:

Now even the time of our youth has been taken:
Now are our deeds words: our lives chronicles:
Afterwards none will think of the night rain....

How shall a man endure the will of God and the
Days and the silence!
                            In the world before us
Neither in Cuba nor the isles beyond —

Not Fonséca himself the sagging whore —
Not the Council the Audience even the Indians —
Knew of a land to the west: they skirted the Floridas:

14

They ran the islands on the bare-pole winds:
They touched the Old Main and the midland shores:
They saw the sun go down at the gulf's beginning:

None had sailed to the west and returned till Córdova:
I went in that ship: Alvarez handled her:
Trusting to luck: keeping the evening before him:

Sighting after the third week land
And no report of a land there in that ocean:
The Indians clean: wearing the delicate bands:

Cape Catoche we called it: 'conës catoche' —
So they cried to us over the sea flood:
Many idols they had for their devotion

Some of women: some coupled in sodomy
So we sailed on: we came to Campéchë:
There by the sweet pool they kindled the wood-fire:

Words they were saying like 'Castilán' in their speech:
They warned us by signs to be gone when the logs charred:
So we turned from them down to the smooth beaches:

The boats followed us close in: we departed:
Afterwards there was a *norlë* with fine haze:
We stood for Potonchán through the boil of the narrows:

There they attacked us crossing the green of the maize fields:
Me they struck thrice and they killed fifty
And all were hurt and two taken crazy with

Much pain and it blew and the dust lifted
And the thirst cracked the tongues in our mouths and before us
      the
Sea-corrupted pools where the river drifts:

And we turned back and the wind drove us to Florida:
There in the scooped sand in the withered bed —
There by the sea they encountered us threatening war:

So we returned to the islands half dead:
And Córdova did die: and we wrote to Velásquez —
Diégo the Governor — writing it out: and we said —

'Excellence: there are lands in the west: the pass is
'Clean sailing: the scuts of the men are covered:
'The houses are masonry: gold they have: baskets

'Painted with herbs: the women are chaste in love' —
Much else of the kind I cannot remember:
And Velásquez took the credit for this discovery:

And all we had was our wounds: and enough of them:
And Fonséca Bishop of Búrgos (for so he was called)
President of the Council: he wrote to the Emperor

16

Telling the wonderful news in a mule's volley
And not a word of our deeds or our pains or our battles:
And Charles gone: and Joanna the poor queen stalled

In Tordesíllas shaking the peas in a rattle:
And Barbarossa licking his chin in Algiers:
And trouble enough in Spain with all that

And the Cardinal dying and Sicily over the ears —
Trouble enough without new lands to be conquered and
Naked Indians taken and wild sheep sheared:

But as for us that returned from that westward country —
We could not lie in our towns for the sound of the sea:
We could not rest at all in our thoughts: we were young then:

We looked to the west: we remembered the foreign trees
Borne out on the tide from the unknown rivers
And the clouds like hills in the air our eyes had seen:

And Grijálva sailed next and we that were living —
We that had gear to our flesh and the gold to find
And an old pike in the stall with the haft to it slivered —

We signed on and we sailed by the first tide:
And we fought at Potonchán that voyage: I remember
The locusts covered the earth like a false shine to it:

17

They flew with a shrill sound like the arrow stem:
Often we took the whir of the darts for the locusts:
Often we left our shields from our mouths as they came:

I remember our fighting was much marred by the locusts:
And that voyage we came to the river Tabasco:
We saw the nets as we came in and the smoke of the

Sea over the bar: and we filled the casks there:
There first we heard of the farther land —
'Colúa' they said 'Méjico' — we that were asking the

Gold there on that shore on the evening sand —
'Colúa' they said: pointing on toward the sunset:
They made a sign on the air with their solemn hands:

Afterward: north: on the sea: and the ships running
We saw the steep snow mountain on the sky:
We stared as dream-awakened men in wonder:

And that voyage it was we came to the Island:
Well I remember the shore and the sound of that place
And the smoke smell on the dunes and the wind dying:

Well I remember the walls and the rusty taste of the
New-spilled blood in the air: many among us
Seeing the priests with their small and arrogant faces:

Seeing the dead boys' breasts and the idols hung with the
Dried shells of the hearts like the husks of cicadas
And their human eyeballs and their painted tongues

Cried out to the Holy Mother of God for it:
And some that stood there bore themselves the stone:
And some were eaten of wild beasts of their bodies:

And none of us all but had his heart foreknown the
Evil to come would have turned from the land then:
But the lives of men are covered and not shown —

Only late to the old at their time's ending
The land shows backward and the way is there:
And the next day we sailed and the sea was against us

And our bread was dirty with weevils and grown scarce and the
Rains began and the beans stank in the ovens
And we soldiers were thoroughly tired of sea-faring:

So we returned from that voyage with God's love:
And they talked about nothing else in the whole of Cuba:
And gentlemen sold their farms to go on discoveries:

And we that had fought in the marshes with no food —
We sat by the palms in the square in the green gloaming
With the delicate girls on our knees and the night to lose:

We that had fought in those lands....

                                    and the eloquent Gómara:
The quilled professors: the taught tongues of fame:
What have they written of us: the poor soldiers:

We that were wounded often for no pay:
We that died and were dumped cold in the bread sacks:
Bellies up: the birds at us: floating for days

And none remembering which it was that was dead there
Whether of Búrgos or Yúste or Villalár:
Where have they written our names? What have they said of us?

They call the towns for the kings that bear no scars:
They keep the names of the great for time to stare at —
The bishops rich-men generals cocks-at-arms:

Those with the glaze in their eyes and the fine bearing:
The born leaders of men: the resonant voices:
They give them the lands for their tombs: they call it *America!*

(And who has heard of Vespucci in this soil
Or down by the lee of the coast or toward the Havana?)
And we that fought here: that with heavy toil

Earthed up the powerful cities of this land —
What are we? When will our fame come?
An old man in a hill town
                    a handful of

Dust under the dry grass at Otúmba

Unknown names
                hands vanished
                            faces

Many gone from the day
                    unspeakable numbers

Lives forgotten
                deeds honored in strangers

'That which I have myself seen and the fighting'...

THE SECOND PART

THE TRUE HISTORY OF BERNÁL DÍAZ

THE ARGUMENT

OF THAT world's conquest and the fortunate wars:
Of the great report and expectation of honor:
How in their youth they stretched sail: how fared they

Westward under the wind: by wave wandered:
Shoaled ship at the last at the ends of ocean:
How they were marching in the lands beyond:

Of the difficult ways there were and the winter's snow:
Of the city they found in the good lands: how they lay in it:
How there was always the leaves and the days going:

Of the fear they had in their hearts for their lives' sake:
How there was neither the night nor the day sure: and the
Gage they took for their guard: and how evil came of it:

How they were dead and driven and endured:
How they returned with arms in the wet month:
How they destroyed that city: and the gourds were

Litter with blood: and they made their roofs with the gun stocks:

Of that world's conquest and the fortunate wars....

· · · · ·

THE FIRST BOOK

SO DOES a man's voice speak from the dream that bears his

Sleeping body with it and the cry
Comes from a great way off as over water —
As the sea-bell's that the veering wind divides....

Now is it Díaz in the Book —

                                ....where

                                              lost in the....

Santiágo de Cuba it was: I remember....

Hoisted over the....

                        king's arms and a cross on it....

Cortés I mean and the pleat of his purse empty:
And they made him captain: Duéro did: and the split-up
Three ways and as for the Governor....

                                 slept....

November and warm in....

                       surf....

                    the dry winter:

Palms ragged with sea-gust....
                    all careened with the
Weed in the rusty chains and the keelsons splintered....

Bleaching with sun and the....
                    nights in....
                         elegant knees like the
Girls in Spain and the sand still hot from the sun and the
Surf slow....
          wind over....
                    palm-trees sweeping the

Stars into darkness....
                    weeks....
                         waited....
                              the guns
Brassy in....
          loading the cobbed maize and the pigs and
Powder enough for a....
                    ropes on the....
                         eight tons:

And we launched the last of them well out and the brigantine
Cocked in the poop like a Genoa....
                         sixteen horses:
Alvarádo's the mare the sorrel the big one:

27

Montéjo's the galled gelding: his rump sore with it:
Puertocarréro's grey that the captain bought him:
A fast dark chestnut horse of de Mórla's:

Ortíz the musician's stallion: well taught:
Clever under the bit: the mare La Rabóna:
The captain's hack that died of the foul water:

Láres the excellent horseman a strong roan:
Gonzálo de Sandovál's La Motílla: the best of them:
A chestnut bearing a white star: and the loan of a....

And we lay by for the beans and they told Cortés....
Governor knew of the....
                              wild and the writ signed
And the sergeants out in the King's square to arrest him:

And the captain heard it at dusk and the wind rising
And he ordered the lot of us down to the ships by dark
And the chains short....
                              bucking the....
                                        all that night....

Sentries at....
                  waked and beachward and still stars and the
Governor riding his white horse on the fish nets
Big in the fault of the light and his men armed

And the palms back of him black and the leaves threshing:
We cold on the dew-wet decks: yawning: our
Mouths sour with sleep: the pimpling flesh

Crawling under the thin cloths: and at dawn the
Captain out in the oared boat: and we hoised the
Jibs on the rest of them: getting the low airs: yawing

Wide to the ruffle of squalls and we cleared the buoys
And we luffed up by the quay with the gear rolling
And Velásquez cried to him there in his bull's voice —

'How is it O my Compadre I see you go?
'Is this the right way to take leave of the Governor?'
Hollow it was on the gale as a conch blowing:

And Cortés below there and the quay above:
And he stood to the swing of the sea in the boat's stern
Baring his head and the tune of his voice like a lover's —

'Señór! there are some things in this sinful world
'Best done before they're thought of! At your orders!'
And they stared across the water with no words:

So did we sail dragging the boat aboard:
And we bought supplies at Trinidad and Havana:
And Velásquez wrote to the said towns and he warned them

Blaming us all: and as for that shameless man
Let them arrest the son-of-a-bitch for a traitor
Shipping him down with the oats or....

                              'given my hand this

'Tenth day of December Fifteen Eighteen':
And they came with the writ in their belts and their mouths
        dumb:
And Cortés was an eloquent man: skilled in orations:

And even the Governor's messenger signed up:
And the town clerk had a quill in the ink for Velásquez —
'That the hare was still as the tuft of a turf till you jumped him:

'And the boar a suckling till you bruised his back:
'And as for the Captain Cortés — Your Honor's obedient
'True man and a loyal tongue and irrascible:

'And better armed than the Constable's guard or the Veedor
'And peaceful at heart: and they feared he would burn the
        town!'
And they sent that off by a nigger for God speed:

And Cortés had a service of sound plate and a gown and a
Gilded knot to his shirt and his chain gold
And a smile for the troops with the orders....

                              month....
                              bound for the....

Burden of pork and we borrowed her rope and we towed her....

THE SECOND BOOK

....So

Sailed we out from the Island to Cozumél:
Winter it was and a wind and a swell rolling

(*10 Feb.
1519*)

And the stain of the foam on the long flank of the swells:
And they gave us the signals for night with the swung lanterns
And the chains came in: foul with the tatters of kelp:

And the bow fell off from the wind and the sails slatted:
Shaking aloft: filling the bunt: the sea furrow
Following under the drawn keel: land

High on the northward and the windy birds:
And they told the pilot: the old man: the Comácho
(Showing him wax on the seal and the ink words)

He should lie-to off the capes and Cortés would catch us:
And he was a sea-going man: a native of Pálos:
One that would trust God — but he'd try the hatches!

He said: 'I'll lie-to when I can't sail!'
And the capes went down and we took the sun for a bearing
Keeping the breeze on her beam: and the windward stays

Stiff in the smoking chocks: in the chains: and the airs
Swung east and the swells came in on the quarter
Kicking her off: and he held her down as he dared:

So it went: and the fourth day and to starboard
A low line like the blur of the wind on the sea
And we worked her in with the oared boats to that harbor:

Shoals there were and the blue channels between them
And the herons rising to the rake of oars
And the wash under the dark banks in the tree roots:

We lay to leeward of that silent shore
And the drip of the dew came down from the slack sails
And the stir of mangroves when the wind was toward us:

All night were the stars above our faces
And the smell blown seaward of that unknown earth:
(The air of the unknown lands has a strange taste to it):

And the next day we....
                    gone and the coals burning
And corn enough in the crocks and the thread to weave
And neither a man nor a dog nor a hen nor the skirt of a

Running girl in the town: and he came that evening
Feeling his way like the blind-man's boy with the cook:
Ten ships on the oars and the anchors reeved:

The leads going like carpenters' hammers: the look-outs
Thick on the chains and the ropes and the spars and the decks
        like a
Sick flock waiting for sun in a rookery:

And he ordered us out of the bags of our beds and he lectured
        us —
'Did we think it was fox and geese we were there playing?
'Did you pacify people taking their gold and their chickens?

'And these were nothing: a poor folk: and our way was
'Far on to the west: and the gold was piled in the
'Open fields in that land: and to learn patience:'

And he sent word to the chiefs it was their island:
And the girls ran in the village like tame boys:
And their breasts were bare and their brown throats and they
        smiled at us:

And the orders of Captain Cortés were not to annoy them....

Trees toss in the....
                dunes: how the surf was dumb the
Inaudible thunder....
                for a Cuban coin

Or a new skirt or a cake....

                how the gulls would come
Drifting to windward: how the wiry turf would
Smell of a strange herb and a strong summer:

I remember the dry leaf shook in the shudder of surf:
I remember the gulls would veer where we were hidden
Wheeling to leeward and the wing-tips curved...

Girl's comb or a....

             sea far out with the tinned
Hazy glitter of gales on it....

                 so was....

                        days:
And the anchors up and they told Cortés there were Indians

Come from the mainland — how they stood amazed:
How they would thumb at a man's beard: and the signs as of
Heavy toil and of bowed backs they had made: and their

Hands to their hearts: and their spittle to their eyes:
And he stared at the dazzle of sun where the day leaned and he
Spoke — 'It may be in the lands behind are

'Men as we are: Spaniards: naked: gleaning the
'Garnered earth for a slave's grist...' and he pulled the
Lug of his lip as his way was — 'for we needed an

34

'Ear to our skulls to sleep among these wolves:
'And the aid of a tongue to our teeth to drive these asses:
'And the slave will speak as his lord: and if God would there
      were

'Ways to be saved in that land:' and he sent Ordás
And two boats and the guides and twenty men
And a cheap chain in a box and assorted brass goods:

And he bound him out for a week: and a letter — 'Gentlemen:
'I am at Cozumél the island: if you that are
'Slaves there in that nation live I send to you:

'My ships will stand to the shore till the eighth noon:
'The price of your hides herewith: God aiding I
'Sail for the land beyond as the sea proves it:'

And six days were gone and the next and they waited
And neither an Indian's boy nor a dog but the shore and the
Bird's wing and the pelican's cry and they sailed and

Crossed and returned: and the wind fair: and we boarded
And broke sail: and the tide was in: and we ran for it
South by the shoals with the wind on the port quarter:

And but for God we had gone: but de Escalánte
Hove to and his ship down and the bread was
Banked all in that ship and her masts canted:

So we returned: God's mercy defended us:
There it was as they watched from the low land
Looking to northward where the shallows ended

An Indian boat came south by the sea channel
Riding the roil of the surf: the stem down:
Standing the stern-lift an old naked man:

Lean he was of his great age and bowed with it:
His hair white on his eyes: his breech clouted:
And he leapt in the suck of the wave where the ship
      grounded:

Wet with the sea: the weed on him: crying out —
And the sound over the surf — 'Diós y Santa...'
And lost as the wave came down: and our men shouted:

And the officers came to the shore: and we all ran:
And they told Cortés and he came and stood and he saw the
Brown skin and he cried — 'Where is this Spaniard?' —

Yes! and the old man on his naked haunches
Crouching as Indians by the surfy shore
Wearing the yellow rag: the lean jaw of him

Grey with the hair-lock: and the sand before:
The sea past: answering — 'I am he!'
He spoke slowly saying the words like a foreigner —

'When I was come to the long sands to the sea
'No sails were riding: the heart failed in me then:
'I said: thinking it: God has forsaken me:

'Now I perceive that God will be my friend:
'I am Jeronimo de Aguilár:
'Priest I was in the time: from Darién we

'Sailed: striking on stones the beams started:
'The wind drove hither: we were seventeen:
'Now in the ending there are two to part:

'Long have I dwelt in the land where your fortune leads
          you:
'I have interpreted many tongues: I have read the
'Painted rock by the roads where the dead are eaten:

'My two hands I have laid in the springs in the beds of
'Water: my tongue in the bitter rinds: I have broken the
'Sweet bones of the hare and she has fed me:

'I dwelt before you in those lands': and he spoke:
And Cortés was dumb and we brought salt for we feared him
And shoes to his feet and an oil and he was clothed:

And we caulked the ship in the one night....
                                        steering by
East and north: and the 4 March: and at midnight

Gale from the....
   wash....
     the boat gone....
        morning veered

South and the swell on it....
        cape called of the Women....
Hove to in a bight with an iron aft....

Bellies of stone and stone breasts and their limbs like....

And standing away out: for the shoals are flat
And the coast a lee coast if you catch a norther
And sand bottom and no stub for the gaff: and the

Smudge of the land up wind: and to west before us
Nothing: the sea-glare and the sunward glass:
And we stood west on the wind and the seventh morning

Wore ship to a shuffle of air and she slacked and the
Sea was brown and the bog-root on the water:
And we of Grijalva remembered the empty casks

And the corn and the river Tabasco and how they had brought
  us the
Roast fish on that shore: and we talked of trade:
And of gold from the god-trees — and instead they fought!

We poled in by the palms and the swamp brayed with them:
And Aguilár in that ship: and he told the mangroves —
Grinding it out — how we meant well and to pay

And to tell them the truth of God to their own advantage:
And they made a noise with their mouths as a mule's let:
And they rattled the rig of their bows: and that was their
      answer:

And the King's notary writing it down: and they sent us
Words enough with the arrows: and we to the waist
Fought in the sea-flow....
              of defenceless men....

Fled and the naked fallen....
            by that gate
Taking the city: and at dusk Cortés:
And he read the oath by a lamp and a proclamation

Saying the town was the king's town to defend and
Die if we must: and the bats went up from the nettles:
Nevertheless there was more done in the end of it....

And the night was in that city: and we slept:
And the doors were stone to the streets: and I was wounded:
I woke with the smart of my throat at the guard's step:

39

The shadow of roofs lay strong along the moonlight:
The surf was faint far off on the sea front:
And my head was clear with the fighting and no food:

And I watched the moths in the moon at their silent hunting:
I thought then — with the pain of my throat and the winter of
Moon over it — fear was in that country....

THE THIRD BOOK

SO CAME we again to the sea water:

And our wounds we laid in the ravel of torn sleeves
Larded — so did we lack all things — from dead men:
And they sent to us over the marshes to make peace:

They were sick of the battles of horses! and that war ended:
And the chiefs came down with a golden dog and some lizards
And five ducks and of gold and the masks of men·

(And the gold in that province is poor and the work flimsy:)
And cloth ('for the common troops: for their excellent services:')
And one score very superior women

('Not for the troops!' — and the town was skinned like a
        turbot!)
Young girls they were and well mannered:
All of them clean: some said to be virgins:

And one was that Malinál of Painalla we Spaniards
Called Marina and loved well: of women
None had more honor ever at men's hands:

41

A tall girl she was and a straight-limbed:
Her face smooth and pleasant to see for an Indian:
Not embarrassed but frank-seeming and simple:

And Puertocarréro had her: and after him
The Captain Cortés: and her own people obeyed her:
And she knew the tongues of Tenochtitlán and of Cintla....

So did we sail on and the noon shade lay
Sharp to starboard: standing to the equal winds:
Water under the bow-wash green: the wading

Keel clean in the eddyless swirl of it: rinse of the
Salt wake slaking the sea: and we came to the
Outmost ocean: and the light was thin

And we saw the mountains beyond in the faint day:
And they sang to him — 'Cata Francía Montesinos!
'Cata París la Ciudad!' as to say

There were the lands beyond where he should lead us:
There were the waters — 'Do van a dar en la mar!'
And the odor of shallow surf was on the sea:

And the wind swung with the light: and we heard the yardarms
Back to a breaking wind and the sails flatten:
And the air came cold against the creaking spars:

Sea ruffled with squalls: ships scattering:
And we held her northward as the weather wore:
Heeling the gusts: her head down: the hoists slatting:

Standing with morning to an island shore:
And the wind was toward us and we knew that place:
We few — Grijalva's soldiers that before

Sailed in those waters where the low sun paces —
We did remember: and with sideways eyes
Sought and yet looked not in each other's faces:

(So do those men upon whose sky arises
Signalled by solemn bells the ominous star
Turn to each other with the same surmise!)

And we stood: and they saw us how our eyes were darkened:
And a voice cried out from the ship — 'Men of Grijálva!
'Veterans! You of the fights! Look to your hearts!'

And we heard them laugh in their hands: and the voice of
     de Ávila
Filling the slack of the surf like a boy's bugle —
'Did they eat the tongues from the root of your throats like
     calves?

'Have they taken the words from your mouths Veterans?' —
    screwing the
Sneer in the twist of his teeth: and the wind suddenly
Fresh out of that shore and the smoke moving:

And the smell under the smoke of the burning blood:
And the bitter odor of death: and Alvarádo —
'Why are you silent Ávila? What have we done to you'....

And we worked in to a....
                fathoms of....
                          shelving bottom
And no hang for the hooks and a leeward shoal:
And he beached us under the banks in the breaking water:

And we built oasts of the wilting weed to our shoulders:
And the heat was great on the dunes: it was Good Friday:
The heat of the sand was strong where the sun rode:

And they brought us bread and the sweet plums were ripening.
There we slept: and at dawn on the second day
When the mist rose from the smother of surf and the light came

Men were among us of other dress and of faces
Proud and with blunt brows: of great stature:
Their garments woven of thread: and they moved gracefully:

And they carried staves in their hands of a green plant:
And they smelled a rose as they came: their Indian servants
Driving the flies from them: lifting the silver fans:

And they turned their faces among us with no word:
And we saw the look in their eyes that they smiled together:
And they bowed and laid their fingers to the earth:

And they brought us gifts as a burden for many men —
A wheel like a sun and of gold and great as a cart-wheel:
And one as a moon in silver: and a helmet

Spilling with....
                    shaped like lions and their parts....
And golden monkeys and a golden....
                              scornful and
Natural looking with stone eyes and the carving....

And all of it worth by weight in the....
                              pesos de oro:
And we could not speak for the wonder of these things:
And he that was first and of fine dress and the lord of them

He stood alone on that shore on the steep shingle
Facing the sea: and he spoke: and the sound was harsh and was
Dry like the cackle of quick flame with the wind in it:

And the girl Marína spoke it to Aguilár:
And Aguilár interpreted — 'Montezúma
'Emperor over the earth and of those stars:

'The sun is toward him and the altering moon:
'He has beheld your shadows in his houses:
'His are the lands: the glass of the sea knew you:

'Now does he send you from his endless thousands
'These and this treasure: in Tenochtitlán
'Armies are harvested like summer's flowers:'

So did he speak and he pointed with raised hand
Westward out of the sun: and Cortés was silent
And he looked long at his feet at the furrowed sand:

And his voice when he spoke was a grave voice without guile
        in it —
'Say that we thank him well: say also
'We would behold this Emperor:' and he smiled:

And the voice of Marína cried in the sea fall
And they stood on the dunes and were still and the sky back of
        them:
And their plumes moved in the wind as the tree tosses:

And he that had spoken — 'Proud and ignorant man!
'Hardly now is your heel's mark on these grasses:
'The grooves of your ships go down to the sea bank:

46

'Already you name that king! West of the passes:
'Westward of Xícho and of Ixuacán
'And the salt plains and the corn plains and the pastures:

'West of the city where the earth-mound stands:
'West of the burning and the woman mountain:
'There is his town: there is Tenochtitlán:

'The clean wave runs among the island flowers:
'Ancient is all that earth: a long-used dwelling:
'The dead are silent in that ashy ground:

'Old are the gods there: — in the stone-made shelters
'Utter the dry bones their unspoken names:
'The locusts answer in the summer nettles:

'None have conquered that land...'

      and they: as they came to us....

'THAT he had no writ nor right to lie in that country:
'That His Honor's commission was well-known — to trade
'And return with it (viz. return with the cash money):

'That His Honor and all their gentlemen's honors had made
'And won and secured (with share for share to Velasquez)
'Adequate quotes and were quit and were well paid for it:

'That their farms were unmanned and their wives as they hoped
          (but the backs of the
'Cuban boys were quick at a man's toil
'And a straw will do to stopple an empty flask:)

'That many were dead of them even now with their loins and the
'Stones and the sticks and the arrows and such tools:
'And they had no ease at all in that war and no joy of it:

'That he ought to return forthwith to the island of Cuba:
'That he (Cortés) was the governor's man to obey him:
'That he had no title to rest as he well knew:'

And more of the like sort: and the Captain played at it
Pursing the nib of a No on his lip: and he started and
Let pass: and he paused as a man persuaded:

And that was the sign: and we of his own party
Pushing the governor's men with our knees — we shouted
And raised banners in air and our naked arms and we

Cried out we were cogged of the dice and were down
And had lost the blood of our lives in a jew's venture
Trading for gold: and here was an unknown ground

And a land to be taken: and as for the sums spent —
What were they to a new land? and we cursed at him
Asking him what we were: what men —

'Did we come to the gate of a ground like this to return from it?
'If he had no writ of Velásquez's hand let him find one!
'Let him establish a king's town for the birds

'Taking his writ from the Emperor Charles and the spiders
'And damned to Velásquez's deed!'
                                        And our speech prevailed with him!
And he founded the town of the True Cross with a sign-post:

And he made a gallows of wood and a good jail
And the rest in ink with an eloquent text for the mortar:
And the jail he gave to the governor's men: and they lay there

Two nights: and their gall turned gilt like a story:
(Ah what a salve is gold to console the mind!)
And the City making him General-in-chief for Wars with a

Fifth (and the lick of the public dish on the side)
Of any and all or gold or goods or discoveries:
He to precede: and so done: and we signed and

Sealed and delivered and gave: and we gave enough!
And even so there was more: for he besought us
Seeing the state of grace he had in the governor

We should enlarge the Emperor's ear with our thoughts: and
Offer our loves: and lay our lives to his measure —
And speak of the Captain Cortés as our hearts taught us:

And so we did as he said: for the wind threshes
And the thrush must dance to the wind: and we drew stems
And it fell to the Captain himself to write: to Cortés:

And he lined the ink on the page: and he cried — 'Remember
          your
'Deeds Castilians!'
                    and the sand was strewn —

'Holy Cæsarean and Catholic Emperor!

'We the least of Your Majesty's subjects: used
'Long to the wave-lift: wind-led: sea-suffered:
'Beached now on this last land: we salute you!

50

'We sailed to westward from the Island Gulfs:
'Bore three days outward on unmeasured ocean:
'Came to the shores before-seen: saw thereof

'Certain and good towns: forests: the land low:
'And we fought them off by day in the tramped straw:
'Thence we sailed westward as the water showed:

'And there came to us down to the grounding sea in the dawn
'Those that uttered a new name! (And our mouths are
'Sick of the standing meats and the stale water —

'For the springs in Your Majesty's lands are a dry drouth
'And the food is an eaten food and still they devour it
'And they drink the drench of their fathers' loins and their
        houses are ·

'Limed with the dottle of dead bones and are sour
'And their speech is fallen to women and old men
'And cheapened and base in the coin and the gilt scoured

'And the shape of a pound will pass at a few pence:
'And our backs are turned from those lands and from these
        waters:)
'And now is the new world toward us in the west!

'We are as men and without food and the daws are
'Feeding before them in the orchards! Now have we
'Found how the way goes up: and the roads lawfully:

51

'North by the rock have we chosen a ships' town:
'With our heels we have quartered the earth for a church and an
    arsenal:
'We have staked the sunrise on the eastern ground:

'Latrines are ditched in the dry shale and a market:
'The house of the judge is squared on the left hand:
'Everything stands as a town should: and the carpenters

'Pencil the oak: the lime burns in the sand-pits:
'Water is channeled with good joints and the vents made:
'Here shall the ships lie in: and we by the lands: by the

'Sun: to westward: marching:... and already
'Mallets have started the loud beams: therefore we
'Pray your aid and arms to our hearts' strength —

'We that to west now: weirdless: by fates faring
'Follow on star-track: trust have we neither now:
'Traceless this ground: by the grazing deer by the hare crossed:

'A king's name to our road: and the beckoning boughs
'Lead but with onward arms to the wind's ending:
'False-followed is moon-path also: the mountains

'Stand long on the stone of the sky like illegible
'Last inscriptions of departed kings:
'The sun misleads us into night: men

'Nameless: secret: of unknown hearts: drink at the
'Streams before us: and abandoned fires
'Flush on our roadways with the morning wind:

'Few we are to march in the great sky
'And the wild swing of the moon and the wandering nations
'Silence before us and the sea behind:

'The sun stands to our west at the endless shades:
'Only the great hope we have of that country
'Heartens our ominous thoughts now: therefore we pray you

'Stay our hands with the arm of your strength: be unto us:
'Take you these lands! — lest the lean swine devour them
'And our deeds be lost in the earth and our times done....'

And he named Velásquez in two words: 'how had
'Fonséca Bishop of Búrgos by God's Grace and
Inscrutable Providence President of the Council

'Pledged to the said Diégo Velásquez his (say)
'Niece and the deal was for loot in the new countries:
'And we that should win them to walk the ruts for our pay!

'And rot in the bleeding fields and die with our guts out!
'The old inherit the earth and the young fatten it!
'After the wounds: after the war's done

'The old ones sit with the itch of their stones and the rattle of
'Age in the rake of their throats like the sleet in the stubble
'Bounding the new-won lands by the bones of the battlefields!

'They weep for the dead with their mouths and the wet comes!'

And we proffered the Captain Hernán Cortés to his love:
'How he was a right man and His Majesty's humble and

'True servant in God and he ought to be governor
'Guarding the new-saved souls and the coast and the profits:'
        and
Praising his good looks: and we wrote enough:

And we signed in the run of our rank and we sent it off:
And the sons of scorpions ran her in to Havana:
And the Island knew in a night: and Diégo coughed like a

Hooked horse when he heard of the heft of the platters
(For all that treasure was borne in the one ship
And little there was with us but the cut and the cantles:)

And he sent with troops and with smooth talk but they slipped
        him
Running it north and east in a good blow
And they sailed the Bahamas Pass by the Pole and the Dipper:

So they came to Tercéra and Cádiz Roads:
And the King was gone and they fell to the Bishop of Búrgos!
But time and our deeds and His debts and the weight of the gold

And the cold and the late spring and the French all worked for
      us:
And His Majesty came to a Just Conceit of the Truth:
And he talked of nothing for several days but our Services:

And Gentlemen praised the cloth: and the silver moon:
And the gold sun: and the monkeys in gold: and the Indians:
And as for the Bishop of Búrgos — at la Coruña

The roofs are green with the rain and the sea wind!

THE FIFTH BOOK

AS FOR ourselves—the ship went out with the evening:
All we knew was the last sun on the sail-cloth:
We stood a long time watching on that beach:

And the low night came in from the sea: and we lay by the
Ashes of grass and the journey of stars went over us:
Slow too from our sleep went out that sail:

And some dreamed of the ship:—and some woke to it!
I was the watch that night: I heard the water
Swirl as an oar would or a great fish roll:

And afterward there was the creak of a rope pulled taut:
And I called: and we beat on the constable's drum: and they ran:
And their heels scattered the quick coals and we caught them—

The bread aboard and the oil and the fish and the lanterns
And water enough for a long voyage in the tubs:
And he judged them there by the flare of their wicks and the fat
        of their

Own oil — 'that the Pilot Gonzálo de Úmbria
His feet be struck from his flanks:' and the thing was done:
And they bungled the blow in the bad light and the drum-beats

And Juan Cerméño and Escudéro were hung:
And Cerméño fell and they choked his chaps in the halter
His face in the sand like a drowned dog's like a drunkard:

And Cortés was sick of the night's work: and he called
And he ordered us out and to take arms and the horses and
March — 'and as for the damned town let it fall to the

'Hurt and the halt and the traitors at heart and their corpses!
'Let flies inhabit it! Why should we breed worms
'With the clean towns to be won and the west before us?'

And more of the like: and we marched by the night surf
Keeping the sand dunes and the water's sound....

And he was a subtle and secret man of his purposes:

We lay at Cempoála the soft town:
And messengers came from the fleet by night and the word was
Four of the brigs were full and the best foundered —

'And what with the rotten pitch and the rust and the worms
'And the wood cracked as it was and the wear of the rigging
'Feared much for the look of the lot but deferred....'

57

And Cortés was astonished and stared like a dumb nigger
And the next day there were more: and the next: and the end
     of it
Nine gone and the tenth a launch and the pick of the

Bleeding fleet for a duck-pond: and he — Cortés —
Still amazed and still talking of Providence!
And that was the break of the back for the Governor's gentle-
     men:

They stood in the streets at night like a French mob
Scaring the Indian girls with their words and their strutting —
'Did he think he was Jesus Christ? Did he think by God

'He could bring them out like a levy of goats to be gutted
'And fed to the idols and burn their ships and their steel was
'Yellow with rain and their guns worse and the country

'Undiscovered and not known and between them
'All the waters of earth and the westward heaven
'Near over the hills and it might be

'The last wall of the world: and they few left and to
'Follow the plunging sun in the uttermost oceans
'And die and be drowned and their souls lost and bereft of the

'Sweet air and the Spanish earth and their ghosts
'Wander forever the waters of no sail
'And no shore but a wind and a wave's motion!'

That was the weight of their wild breath: and they railed at him
Cursing the bed that bore the bum of his mother
And damning his father's fork for an ape's tail

And himself for the two figged get of a goat and the brother of
Whores and a hare's scut and a bull's gear
And a gull and a kite: one first and another:

And he there in the dark of the huts hearing it:
And all at once was their breath gone: and he spoke:
They turned as at the stick crack the scared deer —

'Your Honors are eloquent men but your good-will chokes you:
'The husk of your love is brittle to your teeth:
'You will eat more softly when the shell is broken:

'As for your words — they are true: there is no fleet:
'And you say the land is a dangerous land: it is dangerous!
'That this is the world's end westward: it may be

'This is the world's end and the serpent rages:
'That our steel rots in the rain: Aye! and our skins do:
'That the place of our death is not known: it is strange

'But men die and unknown and the crows think of them!
'That this is an undiscovered and dark land:
'Of doubtful and ignorant gods: peopled by Indians —

'This is an undiscovered and dark land:
'All this that you say is true: but the words of your
'Fear are not true: there is one ship: man her!

'Take what you will of the store: a keel's burden:
'Spain is east of the seas and the peaceful countries:
'The old tongues: the ancient towns: return to them!

'Why should you waste your souls in the west! You are young:
'Tell them you left us here by the last water
'Going up through the pass of the hills with the sun:

'Tell them that in the tight towns when you talk of us!
'The west is dangerous for thoughtful men:
'Eastward is all sure: all as it ought to be:

'A man may know the will of God by the fences:
'Get yourselves to the ship and the stale shore
'And the smell of your father's dung in the earth: at the end of it

'There where the hills look over and before us
'Lies in the west that city that new world
'We that are left will envy your good fortune!'

And he walked between them and went and no man stirred:
And none spoke of the ships again in that army:
And they chewed their tongues in their mouths like shamed
        girls:

THE SIXTH BOOK

SO DID we pray: and took arms: and we marched: and
We left that sea-remembering land and last known
Ocean: bore bones' weight each one and his arms:

Meagerest burden of beggars our backs had:
And we ate of the grain of the grass for our mouths' meat:
Water we found: our bread also was fasting:

Ever before us lay vast earth secret with
Sun with the green sound with the singing of grasshoppers:
The earth was still against our living feet:

No man of us all that knew that land nor the
Way of the trees in it: neither were waters known:
Neither the customs of the wind: our shadows

Entered the silent shadows of the stones:
And the mouse cried in his tongue: the cricket answered:

Ah but the mark of a man's heel is alone in the

Dust under the whistling of hawks!

                        Companion of

Constellations the trace of his track lies!

Endless is unknown earth before a man....

And we marched in the great plain under the sky-star:

Close footing in steep sun: narrowly

Laid we our feet along the wheeling light:

And the plain went up: rock-colored: barren:

Roses and wild plums over the waters:

Far south of us much snow: as in Aragon

Over the level winter: and we caught

Evening in that place: the smoke standing

West with the wind: with few stars: and we saw the

Knees of mountain on the naked land:

Great wall it was on the west: and at daybreak

Climbing: and had the rain up the barrancas:

And had a pass and a town and the troops lay there

Stewing the thin drizzle on green wood:

(And the smell of the smoke is sour in such places)

And we ate nothing or ill: and we ate roots: and our

Bellies were bitter for bread among those mountains:

So did we follow the waters: and we stood

The third day clear of the unequal ground:
Rocks over: snow hard in the crevices:
And the hawks were under us turning and far down:

A man could look for a great space under heaven
Standing above there: he beheld sea water:
He beheld the sun on countries he had left:

That way do they stand on the ships at Sáltes:
The sea opens before and the tide takes them:
They watch the Spanish land and the fields falling:

They watch the ship-road and the drifting wake....

Then came snow from the pass and the wind under it —
The southwest smoking over ragged acre:

The sun like a stale moon with the stringy scud:
We could not see for the swarming cold: and our thigh-bones
Bitten with steel: our beards rimed: stung with the

Strong sleet: weak in the blood from the islands:
And the cloth we had to our ribs was the raw steel:
We coughed in the wind all night by the flat fires:

(This mountain has no descent but to eastward:
The west is level country: as from ocean
Climbing the shadow of the crag the eagles

Wheel into sun and inland and are low
To shallow gorse: their vans run over flowers:
Darkening leaves: the bees start from them: so

Was land to westward level from that mountain —
A withered earth and an unwatered meadow:
The winter's ashes were scattered on cold ground:

This was the wind's dryness: the north that bends the
Boughs up elsewhere with its rain here wandered
In shapes of dust as a ghost and the drought was shed from it:

I say that the whole country moved as on the
Cloudy steel the image of hands passes over:
So on the plain the image of wind wandered:

Neither were wells nor streams but the salt only:
The roads were as tracks: a goat's rut: *despoplado*:
Even the soil had a bitter taste and the stones of it:)

And we came by day among the desert gods:
And we came to the towns at dusk and the dogs yelping
And the smoke of the corn on the coals and the parched pods
        and the

Old men waiting by the shadowy dwellings
Turning the reeds of their necks as they stared among us:
Talking as crows do — 'Look now!'

'And a great battle of men indeed in their hunger!'

'Bearing these arms they march to the King Montezúma!'

'Or are they as gods — each man as a hundred?'

'Nevertheless in Tonochtitlán there is room for them:'

'Ho! Aye! there is room within on the altars
'And without in the ditches of water is much room!'

And they sniggered as children with shut eyes: and they called
      to the
Indian bearers bending their brittle nails
And they made the obscene sign with their mouths mocking
      them:

And Cortés — shouting it — 'Whose is this mountain pale?'
And the old men: changing their voices: shielding their
Lids from the faint light and their fingers shaking —

'Montezúma the king's land! Of our people
'Clear to the sea's edge was the river corn:
'And they came from the west with their hard eyes and their
      eagles:

'Once we were short of spears: once were the fords deep:
'Now they take what they will in the whole land:
'They rut in our daughters' beds: it is evil fortune:

'We have no name of a man now: our ancestors —
'They that planted the orchards: they were Totónacs:
'I that speak this was a free-born man:

'Beware of the land Colúa you that go to it!'

THE SEVENTH BOOK

TO THE place called of the Red Land....
                              and between the
Fields valleys of great depth: and went down and
Marched in the valleys:
                    and the pools were green a

Copper water: and stank: the earth powder:
No stalk of a leaf in all those valleys:
We alone there and the whispering ground:

The great heat of the sun on us: neither shadow:
Neither shade of the cracked rock in that cañon:
The tree of the sun on our necks: the burning saddle:

So came we to strath's end: lanterns:
Cricked walls: heaped plaster: smell of the
Old men: of the straw: the dogs scattering:

The dusk under that street: the moon withheld:
A thin smoke of the moon on the high barranca:
Mountains after those mountains: and
                         these tongues telling us —

These voices — 'There are the Tlaxcaláns!
'There does the way go in by the earth openly:
'And these are a violent and harsh race: and a man may

'March by the sword in their lands: and they fear no one —
'Only they hate the Colúans and wage war:
'And they wear at their wrists the skull-bone of the crow:

'And a man may enter in violence by that door
'And go as he can and march by the strong places
'And pass them by in the sun and with blows and with swords —

'Not by night nor by doubt nor the dark sayings:'

And we slept and woke with the stars above the cañon:
And the moon fumbled the blurred helms: the braziers

Burned in the black of the wind to a man's hand:
And we marched: and the night was westward: and we followed:
And the sky returned to us covering stars:

                                we had the

Light first in the leaves: we saw Tlaxcála
Under the shallows of the sun: we saw the
Grass-fires floating in the windless hollows....

So stood to the mountains for that dawn:
And the trees came out of the night and the light under them:
And he marched us down by the brook by the bracken shaws:

And we chewed the slip of the alder for dry cud:
Dragging the guns: whispering: foot-sound: creak of the
Cracked spoke in the rut: hearing among the

Waters voices as a man were speaking:
Night-smell under the smell of the fern: the light
Rigid with silence in the net of trees:

And a wind touching our mouths: and the grass whiter:
And our hands were stiff with the taut ropes and the lag of the
Oaken fellies and the stubborn withes:

So came we by day to that savanna:
Vast meadow it was: with rush rooted:
Rank with the dock-weed: there the cricket sang:

Wold was that country under heaven: woodless:
A crow's pasture and a bitter ground:
Téhua they called it: stones of that city stood:

There: covering earth: countless: we found them:
And we lay in the scald of the creek and the cane between
Waiting for sunlight: and we heard the sound

As a surf far off in the fog (and the wind weakens
And falls and silence and the slack sail shakes:)
And our ears were deaf with our blood and we could not speak:

69

And we made signs with the swing of our pikes we should break
    them and
Head them off by the pools and to stand west:
And they came like dogs with their arms down: and their faces

Painted and black and with death's eyes and their breasts
Quilted with cotton and their naked arms:
And the hard hammer of sun on the gold: and their crests like a

Squall of rain across the whitening barley —
We that were mortal and feared death — and the roll of the
Drums like the thud in the ear of a man's heart and the

Arrows raking us: rattle of metal: the goad
Stuck in the fat of the hand: and we standing there
Taking the sting of it....
                    No! we were good soldiers —

Nevertheless it was ill weird for a man
One against many on those dangerous plains
And the sea behind and the hills: and we chocked the cannon

Ramming the stone to the stock and the stiff blaze of it
Flat to the grass: burning the gorse with the powder:
Taking them clean in the bellies with link chain:

And they near in the sun: and they took it shouting:
They threw dust in the air: when the smoke lifted
The dead were vanished from the bloody ground....

Then indeed did our hearts fail us to give
All force and the Indians still in their numbers:
The dead gone: the plain dark with the living:

And still Cortés and the horsemen had not come:
And we must have died by the day's end in that meadow:
And our throats were thick with the dust and our mouths dumb:

And even as we were overcome they fled!
They ran in the rut of the field as the flush and the scatter of
Quail out of corn: and we stood and were near death

And we hoped nothing of these things: and the battle
Wheeling to westward: and the fighting ceased
And the swords fell: and suddenly there were the galloping

Horsemen before us the thud and the shuddering beat and the
Shod feet on the turf and the shout and the quickening
Kick of the calk on the clay and the sound of it easing and

Gone by and beyond....
                    that was a victory!
That was a sight to have seen in a man's time!
Domínguez driving the mad horse with the stick of his

Lance straight in the air and his mouth wide:
Alvarádo behind him: the horse of Cortés —
The flea-bitten rump that he had and the froth on the bridle —

On straight legs: scuffing the dust up: crazed with the
Smell of the spatter of blood: his neck twisted —
That was a sight to have seen in a man's days!

And we lay in the dust where we stood: in the bloody litter:
And we had the words in our dry mouths and the wine in us:
And our hearts were big as a bird in a girl's fist:

And we would have slept where we lay....
                                        and they came behind us
Bearing us other war!
                        And we were one
And they were ten to the one of us: and they died:

They fell by scores and they came again by their hundreds:
And the blood of our veins was run in the earth with our vic-
    tories:
Day after day we fought and we always won!

And we sent them word they were well wealed: and to think of it:
And they came again with their crow's cry and their feathers:
And they fought us back in the brake: and our bellies sickened:

And we saw soon how our bodies were near death
And how we should take that battle with our lives
And pass them by with our bare bones into Mexico —

And nevertheless we fought them lest we die:
And they came at last in the mid-watch: the Modórra:
And we saw the maize-field moving in the night:

And we rode them down in the furrows of plowed corn
And the tuft was over a man's knees when he mounted
And the leaves like a lash on his wrists: and we reined the horses

Driving the stiff of the steel to the squealing clouts:
And that was the ending of one war: and they made the
Peace with their backs: and the old men came out to us....

Never were any in all lands that laid their
Loins to the quilt with more comfort than we had
Wounded and sick as we were and our blood faint:

And that was a good and a loyal and true peace:
And they brought us in by their town and their hempen gar-
          ments
Painted and red: and we came by the water trees

And the green look of the land and the girls their arms like
Harvest withes about the shocks of flowers:
And all laughing with words: and they brought us garlands:

It smelled of the sun and of dust in that town:
They sprinkled the dry earth with the odor of water:
The shape of the shadows faded from morning ground:

And we laid us down in the doors where the moon haunted:
The broom-water smelled on the streets of the heat to come:
We woke with our knees across the stones of dawn there....

So was it those days: dead summer: .
The rains off for the year: and clear: and nights like
Nights north in Navarre: no drums to it:

Sun enough and a floor and the rushes dry:
The rattle of wind in the leaves: the sun's shadow
Cool in the corner of noon as a dog would lie:

The long talk in the dusk — 'of us Spaniards:
'Since to believe we were not gods would degrade them....'
Of Montezúma — how were our weapons sand

And our wars were lost in the wind if we sought that nation:
And none had conquered that city with man's arms:
And they themselves in their time had thought to take it:

And they took dust: and the drought to their mouths: and the
    smart of the
Smoke in their gullets for all good:
                                    of Cholúla —
How was it treacherous thin earth and artful

And false and with gods unsure: the dead ruled it:
And nevertheless there was way west by that city:
But as for themselves the wells of their eyes were fooled with the

74

Shadows of sorrow in that place: and the spittle of
Dreams in their eyes as a sleight: and their fathers knew this:

And we marched by day to the south and we saw the hill
And the god's flame on the hill and the town Cholúla....

THE EIGHTH BOOK

THE falsifiers of things seen!
                              the defamers of
Sunlight under the name of our sky!
                                   and we slew them:

And who are ye to be judge of us? Ye that say....

And their treasons were open and shameless and many knew
        them:
And they thrust their hands through the guises of this world as a
Negro's hand in a girl's breast: and they drew the

Truth as a bee's-comb from a wall to serve them:
And the world they said was a dream and a stale:
        and they offered us
Sadness to suck for our thirst — as a maker of words to an

The Massacre at Cholúla

Idle woman at dusk that her heart be softened:
And they would have destroyed us in that place: the debasers of
Leaves! of the shape of the wild geese on the waters!

Calumniators of evening! priests! betrayers of
Light in the hood of our eyelids! they that discredit the
Silence of death on the dry mouths — and they trace the

Sign between the eyebrows of the dead:
Maligners of evil they were: of the pure ill
Like a crystal of quartz in the heel where the flesh will tread it!

And they told us Tenochtitlán was a whitened filth and a
Great guilt in the air: and deception: and falseness:
And filled with the salt of the dead as a reed with pith:

And they themselves had beheld it —
                                        and we saw their
Eyes like sorcerers and the uncertain
Shadows behind them on the height of walls:

And they said to us — 'Have you not known?   Have you not
        heard?'
And they said 'Has it not been told you from the beginning?'
'Has it not been said from the founding of the earth?'

And they said we should enter and come and lie within
And dwell in trust and with faith sure —
                                        and we knew the
Odor of death on their tongues as a thawing wind!

And we caught them under the cleanness of dawn:
                                        and we slew them!

And who are ye to be judge of a man's fault?
They stood about us in the town Cholúla

And the sun was under the sill of the east and he called to them
Shouting the words out: (and the stones were wet —
I see the young-leaved morning on that wall)

'Was it the loyal love of their hearts that sent them
'With such smiling and glad mouths? Or perhaps the
'Poles they had cut for our necks and the withy pens!

'Did they come to deliver our feet from the falls and the traps
'And the barricados of stone they had built? In what god did
        they
'Trust for reason?   Let them trust the grass!

'For indeed he had read in their hearts as a split cod
'And he knew their souls by their slime as a snail his journey —
'How they had salt for our flesh and a boiling pot:

'But that which our hands should pay them they had earned!'

And they cried as sheep to be sheared and some confessed it:
And the fault was their lord the great king's: and to turn our

Wrath upon Mexico: there was the string stretched:
And Cortés on the stone and the sword drawn — 'Now had they
'Done with words? For the tongues in their mouths were of
        dead men!'

And even then they would smile for their hearts could doubt
     him:
They stood as deer in thicket and the sun
Puzzled their eyes with the blenk and their heads were down....

Afterward they were blind with the raw blood:
They died slowly with much pain like serpents:
Our hands were lame with the sword when the thing was done...

And who are ye to be judge of us...?

THE NINTH BOOK

'THE road back has been covered with many winds:
'The pinch of the five toes in the dust is illegible:
'Before us are other lands and a new winter:

'(Already on rusty quills are the crows threshing:)
'Nevertheless we go on: we are not returning:
'Strange as it is that men: wanderers: wretched:

'Deceived often: misled: their way lost: thirsting:
'March on in the sun! But so the desire has
'Strength over us... and the love the love of this earth....

'(All the crows of the sky have crossed our fires:
'It is a bad sign: a chill winter: dangerous:
'At this season they fly high-up and in silence:

'Their shadows vanish like years on the flat plain:)
'And we that are strong: we march on descending the
'West with evening: and the leaves of sage

'Taste in our mouths of the labor of living men:
'We have bitten the acid oak and the harsh holly:
'We have said — "This is a good land! we will dwell in it!'

'(But who has trodden the way the crows follow?)
'Like the nail of a woman in love is the twig's smart
'Stinging the lips!'
                    And we came by the land and the col:

And we took the willows for night once and the farms:
(The stars over stubble) and we took the snow:
We took the cold for the one night and the larches:

When we were come to the pass and the down-going
That land was under us! There were the longed-for skies!
We stared as drunken men in dusk: as those

That watch for Teneriffe: and the sun rising
Raises that mountain and they stand amazed
Seeing the mark so near them and so high:

To speak clearly with right words I say the
Land lay at our feet as a close or orchard
That keeps within walls and is green and the plow labors:

Not with another ruggedness nor more the
Rock encircles as they say that water
Where the chafing Rhone lies silent on his shores

Than there those mountains: and we saw the straw
Cut in the swaths and gilt and the valley still as
Meadows in July sun where the bees throng them:

(O living-kindness of God's love that permitted our
Sinful eyes to behold these sights and wonders!
How have we thanked thee with words even! how little!)

And we marched down by the hoed fields in the sunlight:
We had forgotten the hunger and hard days:
The town lay on the lake like sleeping gulls:

The stone dyke divided the water: tasting the
Liquor of melons we marched by the lake road:
The king sat on his gold chair awaiting us:

They bore the sun at his forehead on willow poles:
Nobles and lords of that rich land supported him:
Even the straps of the shoes of his feet were golden:

So we were brought between the posts of morning:
And he turned and he stood in the gates and he said smiling —
'Malinchi! these are your houses: these your doors:

'Yours and your brethren's: you may rest awhile:'

THE TENTH BOOK

O HALCYON! O sea-conceiving bird!
The bright surf breaking on thy silver beaches

And the life goes out of us leaving the chucked sherds!

Leaving an old man's memories to leach
Like a cock's jewels of gravel and worn thin
With the sleepless caul of the heart and hard and clean:

Leaving within the eyes behind the fingers
Back of the soft lid and the scarlet vein
The harsh flash of the steel where the light lingers!...

Leaving the slag in us....
                    leaving us those days....

And I see well as from dark into light lying here:
The lint of the broom-straw turns in the sun's ray:

The cocks sing in the heat: there are cakes frying:
The drinking water drops from the hung gourd:
The rafters circle with the dozing flies:

83

The dogs rise and cross to the cool of the urine:

I see well in the dark of the room — as through shutters the
Sun is white on a street and the shadows sure —

As men move under tree-boughs and the sunlight
Leaps like a cat on their gilt capes and clings
And is swept off by the next branch: shunted....

So I remember it: yes: and the evening bringing the
Doves down from the air: their wings steep to it!
And thou Colúa! and the paddles rinsed in the

Clear pools of thy sun! I cannot sleep for the
Light under my lids of thy bitter water:
I cannot sleep for thy cries and the walls keeping the

Leaning weight of thy sun by night and the autumn
Smelling of flowers as spring does: (wearing the
Cotton sleeves we were drunk and the wind caught in them):

And the girls they gave us for love with the scented hair:
The green light through the leaves: the slow awakening:
How there were many and small birds in the air then....

We were like those that in their lands they say
The steers of the sun went up through the wave-lit orchards
Shaking the water drops and those gold naked

Girls before them at their dripping horns!
And they ate the sea-doused figs with the salt taste:
And all their time was of kine and of sea and of morning:

So did we lie in that land in the long days:
And they gave us a king's house to our heads and we dwelt in it:
And the house was smooth and of clean walls and so spacious

And well made and with lime and the stone set there was
Place for us all and the guns and our goods and our Indians:
Each man his mat under him smelling of

Lake grass and of leeks and an ell in width
And his painted cloth with the corn and the cones and the aloes
(For in that land there were men skilled in these images —

Such as sit with a day's sun in their laps
And they stare in the eyes of the trapped hare in the stubble:)
And the rooms smelled of the sweet wood like a chapel:

And all were of plank and were ceiled and of pinned lumber
And painted with scarlet beams and their out-walls burnished
And made to shine as a good coin: and some were

Built to the water and the light returned
And spilled up from the float of the ripples and ran on the
Wall's glare as a flame where the sunlight blurs it:

And some were shadowed to the cool canals:
And they poled in with their slow skiffs and their melons
Leaning against the gaff's end and the slash and

Drip of the stroke came back: and the cries sending the
Sun-bright birds up — and the beat of sound
Would pass and float on the stream and the wings settle:

(For all the isle was channeled as that ground
That takes its stars from Istria and their eyes
See first the new moon toward the Tuscan Mountain:)

And the town rang with the clang of oars and the cries:
And they brought the corn through the water-streets and the
        faggots:
They poled in with the heaped fish: the hides

Smelling of oak: the bowls slobbered with maguey:
They stood in the cool of the dark arcades in the market:
Many there were of them: tall men with the hank of the

Coarse skein on their wrists and their thumbs parting it:
Sellers of split fruits: of blue stones:
Of brass: of the nubile slaves — their hands bargaining:

Stroking the breasts up: and the thing was shown:
Merchants of sweet nuts and of chives and of honey:
Of leaves of dock for the eyes: of a calf's bone for the

Gloss of the hair as the hand draws it: of dung
For salt for the tanning of leather: sellers of yarn:
Old men with the sun-bleached hair and the bunches of

Herbs: of lettuces washed cool: of garlic
Dried brown on a withy of plaited grass:
Sellers of cooked dough by the coal-fires larding the

Stained skirt with the spittle of burning fat:
Those the makers of ropes: those that shredded the
Silken down of a seed and their fingers fastened the

Stone to the twist of it turning the scarlet thread:
Sellers of good dreams: of blue clay for the
Baking of gods: of quills of the gold: of hennequin:

Sellers of beetles for red dyes: makers of
Stone masks of the dead and of stone mirrors:
Makers of fortunate knots: magistrates in the

Swept porch — and they kept the names of the year:
They took the tax on the red stones and the herons:
They judged of the levies of salt: venders of syrups:

Of harsh drugs for the old from the coupling of hares:
Of dry seeds: of sweet straws.... many and
Strange cries that they had.... and they stood wearing the

Knotted and white cloths like capes and they went with
Strong knees through the heat of the sun and their thighs were
Straight and their bellies like knuckles of bronze: and they set
  their

Heels in the sand of the earth as a man riding a
Wave's back in the sea and their sex was naked
And stained with the salt of the sun like a golden hide:

And the tall girls there were in the wind and the way of the
Sun was under their knees and the way of the wind
Like a hand over them: smoothing the scarves out: shaking an

Odor of noon from their skirts like the odor at midday of
Clean cloths to bleach on the water stones
(And the butterfly opens his slow wings:) and their skin like the

Rain's fragrance of water: (one alone
Returns from a shadow of plantains and her mouth
Secret with lust as the honey of black combs):

And their loins were heavy with love and they laid them down
Under the lids of their eyes as under a garment:
They gave themselves in the green herb and the flowers:

Ah how the throat of a girl and a girl's arms are
Bright in the riding sun and the young sky
And the green year of our lives where the willows are!

How they were slender with strong breasts and the light of the
Leaves over them! How there were tall men
And the wading lake to their wrists and their wet thighs

Dabbled with sunlight: and they drew the nets
In the green sedge of the shore and they came singing:
The sea-film silvered in the lifting web:

Ah how the land was a good land! and the king of it
Rich and with young wives and with gold and his gardens
Sounding with water: and he went to drink

At noon at the grooved stone by the sheds and the jars were
Choked with the float of the sun: and he ate simnel
And sweet cakes he ate and a kind of partridges:

And none knew his ways or his times with women:
Silent he was and not seen and he came by
Dark: and his desire was in their limbs as an

Odor of plums in the night air and they wakened
Stretching their arms out and between their knees
Delight like the sun's mouth and the water's weight:

And all his house was sounding as of trees
And the leaves of the trees were dark and a dew came down from
        them:
Even at noon the dew fell like an ease of

Dusk to comfort a man's eyes: and the ground was
Trodden with naked heels: and he kept beasts:
And birds he kept in a grove and the green loud with the

Locusts and golden and shrill wrens and the bees
In the split hive of the wall and the names of serpents
Curled in the painted vessels at his feet:

And he kept marks on a stone for the sky's turning —
For the way of stars in the trees and the moon's toil:
Niter and salt he ate from the quick earth:

They brought baskets of sweetened seeds and of oil to him:
They cried to him Lord! my Lord! my great Lord!
They came with naked feet and the small voices:

Ah how the land was a good land! and the doors with
Morning with many leaves with the clean odor of
Water sluiced on the night stones: (and the core of the

Broken melon smelled of a girl's robe:)
We woke scenting the slot of the heat on the air:
We rinsed our mouths in the sun: by the listed boats

Purging ourselves to the coarse sand the glare of the
Sun was a cleanness of pebbles: far out
The fisherman leaned to his line and the silent herons:

And we lay under a lift of the green and their gowns were of
Spun twist in our hands: the hollow groin
Beat with a small heart: we heard the trowels

Strike on the brick of the roofs like silver coins:
We heard the whistle of tamed birds: to our tongues
Our mouths were sweetened with the scented ointment:

And we drank of the milk of the aloe and were drunk:
And the words hived in the heap of our bones and we praised the
Taste of a bitter leaf: we praised the sun

And the earth for the odor of men in its hot days —
For a woman's color of pink shell or the pock of the
Purple vein at her breast as a bruise made in it:

We praised the trampling of sun as a gilt cock:
Our hearts were singing as hammered bronze and our mouths
        with
Sound as the corn is where the wind goes: and we mocked the

Shape of love with our thumbs: we cried aloud of the
Great sky: of the salt rock: of the land....

And nevertheless it was not so: for the ground was

Silent against us: on our foreign hands
The dust was a solemn and red stain: our tongues were
Unskilled to the pulp of their fruits as a language of

Sullen stones in our mouths: we heard the sun in the
Crackle of live trees with the ears of strangers....

And they passed with their cries at dawn and their deep drums:

And we saw them go by the stone courts and the cages:
And all clean and with coarse lime and the temple
Steep in the reach of the sky...

                          and the boy was slain!

The belly arched to the stone knife: I remember
They sang and were glad as a small child in the sunlight
And they ate the limbs for a feast and the flesh trembled....

THE ELEVENTH BOOK

THE smoke for a sign my people as the churn of
Crows above death's burning on the beach....

And the shadow of terror arises on this world as a
Cloud out of the north-east: and death is
Everywhere like a resemblance....

                                       sleeping we heard the

Sound of the lake in the water streets that weather:
Waking we thought of the narrow dyke and the bridges!

Ever behind us by night was the water's breath:

Before us: uncovered in the windy ditch: their
Teeth uttering slow sand the slain
Unnumbered dead were dumb and their eyes hidden:

Hearing the ceaseless waves we were afraid!
We rose in the dark of the mid night with no stars:
We cried to the walls of the town we were there waiting!

The lake-sound answered us! fools — we wished in our hearts to
Live in the land and the town safe and secure in it:
We thought in our fear their king should be our guard —

'Why should we suffer the dark chance or endure the
'Skill of the moon on our dreams or the fortune's changing?
'Seizing this king the silences were sure!'

And we marched down by the torches in dark way:
And we found him under the garden trees and his shoulders
Shone in the torchlight in the leafy rain:

He stood there: answering —

                                  '.... gladly if to go
'Now were our ordinance: for we were men
'Sent from before-time: and the thing was known

'Long since in his land and his doors were ready:
'We were those men they knew of that should come:
'And therefore our terror was ill-taught to defend our

'Bodies and fear death: for death was dumb
'And mute and of lawful life as an herb or as beasts or
'Rain is: and savage as stones: and humble:

'And death also was ours and our bread and to eat as
'One out of many corns: and as one among them
'Tasting of silence and of smoke and peace:

'Seeing the bones of a man have many hungers
'And need death as the doe salt: and fear is
'Witless among us and its cricket tongue

'Thin as the whistle of dry straw and as tears of
'Salt dried on a stone for bitterness: let us be
'Warned and taught of the true word and to hear the

'Birds of death in our trees as the god sent them:
'Neither to stand in violence and with force:
'For we came to his house with loud cries and as enemies!

'How should it serve our fortune to make war
'Or to bind his limbs with our steel? Though our metal held him
'How should we hold death? There were many doors:

'And a man spills from the cup of his bones as spelt —
'From the shape of stone on his wrist as running water:

'Nevertheless he would follow as we led:'

And Cortés was wild with the night's work —

                                        'had we brought the
'Whore of death to our beds and our house to serve us?
'How should we profit by these deeds? And we thought our

'Ills were done! And the wheel of our luck turned!
'And the toss was tamed to our hands! But it was not so
'But evil fortune and the last and worst and

95

'Great fault of those wars!'
                                and so as he spoke the
Die fell: and we lost our lives: and we lost the
Land for it after: and the town was sown as

Dry salt with the bitter seed: and with slaughters
And much death in that house: the thousands slain....

Sleeping among those walls we heard the water
Treading behind us with its ceaseless waves.

THE TWELFTH BOOK

WHEN have the old forgiven us these things
Or the new lands or the sun on them?

.... we being lords in that town and our hearts insolent!
And the word came up there were ships hove-to in the offing:
And we knew well the Governor's men had the wind of us:

And we knew Fonséca was rooting in that trough —
The fat brach that he was: the breeding monk's-head:
And Velásquez was in it with two tongues and the soft of the

Fry in his bib like a glibbed boar in a bucket:
And their writ came up by the road with the ink sanded —
How we were traitors before God and His Son and the

King Charles and the Holy Church and the Spaniards and
Him Bishop of Búrgos and him Velásquez
And one thousand four hundred they had of the

Brave Biscayans and horses and all that brass
And the new bows and the iron balls and the powder:
How we had entered without law nor with act nor

97

Writing nor good writ nor with warrant: how we had
Crossed seas to that land and had made discoveries:
How we had marched to the new west and had found a

New nation of new tongues and had suffered a
Strange land and ways and wars and had dwelt with them:
How we were traitors and lacking in right love

And right care of our own kind and begetters of
New sorts as we were and inventors of wind
And our souls guilty as his was that in Hell

The horned flame muffled and his voice within —
'And as for our pride in our great deeds we should swallow it:
'Nevertheless they accepted our lands for the widows!'

And he called us out on the Square — such as would follow him:
And Alvarádo he left in the armed town:
And we marched east by the hills to Cempoála:....

The Biscayans they were! — and we brought them down!
And they fought us the one night in a wet rain:
And we were the fewer of men's names but they counted the

Sparks of the flies for our gun-matches: and they were
Ten to the one of us: and as for matches —
As for powder we used pikes: and lame with the

March down: and we set the flame to the thatch and they
Fell like the burning bees where the winds toss them:
And Narvaez (he was my Lord's man of Velásquez

And Captain-General of that lot and he lost an
Eye by a light spear and he lay fettered)
He cried to Cortés in his vault's voice — 'to have fought

'And won with unequal numbers — he must send it a
'Great feat of his arms!' and Cortés answered him —
'As for winning he thanked God and these gentlemen:

'But as for the taking of him (Narvaez) that was the
'Least thing he had labored in New Spain:'
And he made them a speech from the drums and they changed
      masters:

And the field was ours and the land and our lives safe in it!
And we lay in the meadows with no watch: and our pride was
Ripe as wine in our hearts: and we slept —
                    and the day was

Not yet dark on the hills when the luck denied us!
For the news came down of a great war on the causeway —
How they had opened the dry ditch and had prised the

North door by the gelding's stall and the hause was
Heaped full of their dead and of ours seven:
And Alvarádo had written it —

                        'As for cause there was

'No cause but a trap and the fools had set it:
'And they came in on a clear day to dance:
'And he gave them the usual king's writ to assemble:

'And they left their arms in a priest's house in the passages:
'And he saw they were many and great chiefs and he knew the
'Plumes they had were of war: and he saw their plan:

'And he locked the gates: and the guns and the corporals slew
      them:
'And nevertheless they were made mad by that slaughter:
'And they came like wasps in swarms as the wind blew:

'And the ways were full of their slit mouths and they fought like
'Wild dogs: we should ride well if our tongues would
'Talk to his living ears for he lacked water:'

And Cortés was dumb with his rage and he walked among us
Praying to God to punish a violent fool!
And Alvarádo should bleed and burn and be hung for it:

And he swung heel to the mare and marched and at noon it was
No stay but to stand nor at dusk neither
Nor rest by road-side: and the time was June

And late light in the loft air: and the evening
Smelling of sad leaves and we marched casting a
Thin shadow as glass: and the road beneath us

Leading as last year's road by last year's passes:
But the look of the land was changed from the last year:
And the towns empty and changed and the cook-wood scattered:

The kettles blackened with the charring ears:
And we saw their smokes on the near hills for our coming:
And our way went up with the smokes: and our bellies feared it

Hearing the Spanish metal and the drums
And the dry bleat of the wheels and the silent mountains!
And nine days out of ten the nags stumbled:

And the tenth Colúa: and we saw that ground:
And there where the throngs were once along the gardens
Now did the bird rise from the shaken bough:

And void wave where the boats were then: and dark: the
Sea-slap only and the late bird's wing:
The night: the windless water bearing stars:

And we marched in by the hard road: and the ring of
Stone to hoof-shoe was the iron sound:
And we saw walls in the bat's light and a blink of

Lamps and entered and our own were round us
Whispering words: their mouths white by the lanterns:
The swung light upward on the jut of brows:

Meager they were in the small light: a man could
Taste the salt of their tears on their silent tongues:
Their eyeballs glittered to the gunner's matches:

And the place smelled of the doused ash and of hunger and
Sick men's nights and of death: and the dead were slack in the
Bloody straw of the earth as a coat is slung: and he

Said (Alvarádo) 'The Captain's back!
'It's a quiet city Captain!' and he: hoarse —
'And a green grove for apes and a jakes for jackals!

'And not so did I leave this town!' and he bore the
Mare round on the short rein and he left him:
And we weary with long way and the swords like

Scalds across us and the heavy metal:
We were the sleepers leaning where we could:
And we lay down as the dead do under heaven:

And the walls above us: and the watchmen stood:
And nevertheless there was no sound in that city —
Only the roaches in the blistered wood:

Only the she-mouse hunting in the thistle:
We laid us down as dead men and we slept:

... eyelids covering many stars....

THE THIRTEENTH BOOK

                    ... And this was

Late watch of that sky and the Ram was set and
Night lay westward with her stars:
                                    and waked
Foolish with sleep with a man's cry and the step of

Steel on cope-stay: and the day was breaking
Bringing the water smell along the stones:
The Pole Star faded from the fading Wain:

And we woke in the straw in the half light: and León was
There above us on the brink of wall:
And Sandovál: and the silence....
                                    and we rose

And we went on the wall by the three rungs and we saw it!

Mother of Heaven there were many men!
Even in Spain at Sevílla when at dawn they

Pray and the bread is broken and the tens and
Thousands stand there in the narrow streets
And they kneel down to the bells are not so many —

Neither so silent! and our eyes could see them
East and south by the great square and their crests were
Floated in lake-fog: and their naked feet

Hushing the earth: and stood: and when the west was
Light the faint stir....
                         and they saw the sun!

Mother of God! in age now: forgetting the

Wars in Mexico and all men's tongues and
Cries and shouting and the clamorous words I
Hear those voices shouting and those tongues!

And they came like wolves in the streets: and the water birds
Rose with the shouting: and we heard the wind in the
Shrill nipple of stone as a wasp: and we heard the

Slings as scythes and the deep drums and they kindled the
Cook-room walls to the up-wind and the court was
Strawed with their throws as a threshing floor: and we killed them

Hacking their hands from the scarp: and there came more:
And they tore their hands on the slash of the steel but they
        reached us —
We that were lame with the weight of our own swords:

And only night was our aid then: and for sleep we
Pleached roofs with the rack of the spears: and we knew there
      was
No help but the king's help or to flee for it:

And our mouths were bitter with the bloody rheum:
And we stood by the kettles and many were near death
And our wounds cold and we talked of Montezúma:

And we called his name from the burned sheds:
                       and Cortés was
There among us eating and he spoke —
'That we save our throats for sucking up our breath!

'That we keep our mouths for the meat seeing there go to
'Death journeys of such haste! that our fault was
'Then when we took this God's-butt for our hold and

'Pledge and hostage: that our fears had brought our
'Fears upon us: and had lost the town:
'And our lives were to lose if they circled the west wall:

'That the laws of this land were foreign and not ours
'And they laid death as a wafer on their tongues
'And he had no hope of the harvest of that ground:

'That men were fools to take the god among them:
'For a man's part is to labor and fear death
'And die in pain as he must and in his hunger:

'And the gods were of other lands: nevertheless
'As our will was: and our wisdom: let us do....'

And the smoke coiled on the cold stones: and we went by

Dawn on the wall-head there: and Montezúma
Clad in the gold cloth: gilded: and he smiled:
He climbed by the stair and smiling and they slew him:

He stood on the stone in the gold in the first light
And the war below: and they fought like dogs in the ditches
Whistling and shrieking: and we heard a sigh as the

Sound in leaves when the storm ends and the pitch of
Rain runs over and far on and the wind is
Gone from the willows and the still leaf drips:

And all at once there were stones and the sky hidden:
And he stood in gold not falling: and he fell:
The lances blurred in the sun as a wheel spinning:

His eyes were lewd with the strange smile: and they yelled as
Fiends in Hell and as beasts: and when we thought it
Least for the bitter fighting he was dead:

All that day and into dark we fought:
And we lay in the straw in the rank blood and Cortés was
Hoarse with the shouting —'... for a man was wronged and a

'Fool to suffer the Sure Aid but to best it and
'Fight as he might: and he prayed all of us pardon
'And grace if he spoke our hurt: but we were men:

'And we saw well what weapon was our guard: .
'And now there was none: only the night: and the ways were
'Barred before us and the ditches barred

'And the dykes down by the banks and the water-breaks
'Open and armored and they held the roads:

'And nevertheless we had the choice to take them!...'

THE FOURTEENTH BOOK

BY NIGHT: by darkness: turning from the sun....

And he ordered us out by the south wall and the horsemen —
'And none were to follow him grudging by that road:
'And no man's name was needful to those wars

'For the women in Spain have borne and still bear soldiers....'
And de Ávila answered him — 'Soldiers and captains too:
'And we well deserved that he should tell us so!'

And he ordered the gold from the stone-room for the troops:
And Narvaez's people were weighted as great lords:
And nevertheless there was mettle enough to lose of it —

Seven hundreds of thousands of pesos de oro
And the pelts of birds and the jade and the painted cotton —
The rape of Mexico: the riches of that war —

And it lay in the sift of the ash and men's feet trod it:
And he ordered a bridge of planks for the broken causeways
And men to bear it: and they drew the lots

And we lined up in the dark court and the straws were
Drawn by candle: and we saw the rain for the
Flame spat to the wick: and León had lost and

Alvarádo: and they swung the gate
And we marched out by the still street and the smell of the
Rain was rank with the rotting blood with the taint of it:

We talked little in that time: ahead the
Walls came toward us with the marching feet:
And the street turned and the sound fell: we held the

Metal muffled: and a man could see to the
Man's shape before in the rain: and still there was
No sound but our own and the town was sleeping:

And we knew the causeway by the water silt:
We heard the rain in the reeds....
                                    and the rear-guard halted
Sending the word up that the planks were split

And the bridge bogged at the last break — at the water —
And all that a man could do they....
                                    and we heard the
Sedges sliding: and we heard a call

And a call beyond and fainter as of birds
Waked in the rushes: and again the rain and
Silence and the water sedge: and the word was

Wild among us and the bridge still stayed:
And one Botéllo: a bowman: a maker of charms —
And they found in his boxes after as a shape of

Hide and of flock-wool: stuffed: as a man's parts:
And a book with signs and written — 'Shall I die?'
And afterward — 'Thou shalt not die!' and farther —

'Shall I be slain alas in the sad fighting?'
And under it — 'Thou shalt not!' and again
'So shall my horse die also?' and the sign —

'Yes they will kill it!' — and this fool Botéllo
Crying beyond in the night and his voice hoarse —
'Sorrow I see like smoke of rain descending!

'Death's seal is made in the flesh of your foreheads:
'Your limbs Oléa lie in a shallow sod:
'I too....'
                    and we heard de Mórla's horn

And the rear-guard answering and Alvarádo:
And all at once there was some word they were shouting:
And the ranks were broken: and we cried to God

Driving the fore-guard on: and the bridge was out: and the
Stones were shrill in the thick air and the arrows:
We saw the water where the dykes went down:

We drove as cattle drive against the barriers
Bearing before us: and the plunging horse
High on the heap: and the wheels: and the dyke narrow:

Blinded with darkness: and the ditch before....
(*They fell in the road and were not raised: their cloaks*
Muffled the stone: in their hands were their broken swords:

In the ditches of water they drowned and the sand choked them:)
We struck their arms from our knees in the blind fighting:
By the dead we came over: and the dead were most:

And the morning light was rising on that sky:
And we came to the land there: and we saw the lake
Silent and under mist and the city lying

Lost and behind us as a man should waken....

And we were but few men standing and the rest to come:
And we saw where five came toward us: their heads naked:

Running: bloody with many wounds: and one was
Alvarádo with the stumbling step:
And after these was the road: and no man other:

And the morning rose and the low sun: and we wept
Seeing so few alive that left so many:
Seeing that once-loved city....

Yes!

and we set our

Eyes to northward: and León was dead
And Láres and de Mórla and there died of
All eight hundred and the powder spent:

The guns gone: the gun-men gone: to ride the
Wounded horses: to eat earth: drums in the
Ear of the night in the yellow lands beside us:

And the whistling and jeering: and they held the scrub:
And they drove us up in the dust with the jack spears:
And they herded round us in the field Otúmba:

And the plumes sawed in the sun like maize: and we feared
    them and
Fought blind and with God's grace we came out of it:
And we lay beyond the mountains for that year....

THE FIFTEENTH BOOK

CONQUISTADOR....

And we marched against them there in the next spring:

And we did the thing that time by the books and the science:
And we burned the back towns and we cut the mulberries:
And their dykes were down and the pipes of their fountains dry:

And we laid them a Christian siege with the sun and the vultures:
And they kept us ninety and three days till they died of it:
And the whole action was well conceived and conducted:

And they cared nothing for sieges on their side:
And the place stank to God and their dung was such as
Thin swine will pass for the winter flies and the

Whole city was grubbed for the roots and their guts were
Swollen with tree-bark: and we let them go:
And they crawled out by the soiled walls and the rubbish —

Three days they were there on the dykes going —
And the captains ill of the bad smell of that city
And the town gone — no stone to a stone of it —

And the whole thing was a very beautiful victory:
And we squared the streets like a city in old Spain
And we built barracks and shops: and the church conspicuous:

And those that had jeered at our youth (but the fashion
        changes:)
They came like nettles in dry slash: like beetles:
They ran on the new land like lice staining it:

They parcelled the bloody meadows: their late feet
Stood in the passes of harsh pain and of winter:
In the stale of the campments they culled herbs: they peeled the

Twigs of the birch and they stood at the hill-fights thinking:
They brought carts with their oak beds and their boards and the
Pots they had and the stale clothes and the stink of

Stewed grease in the gear and their wives before them
Sour and smelling of spent milk and their children:
They built their barns like the old cotes under Córdova:

They raised the Spanish cities: the new hills
Showed as the old with the old walls and the tether of
Galled goats in the dung and the rock hidden....

Old.... an old man sickened and near death:
And the west is gone now: the west is the ocean sky....

O day that brings the earth back bring again

That well-swept town those towers and that island....